Ornithopods

Two-Footed Dinosaurs

by Grace Hansen

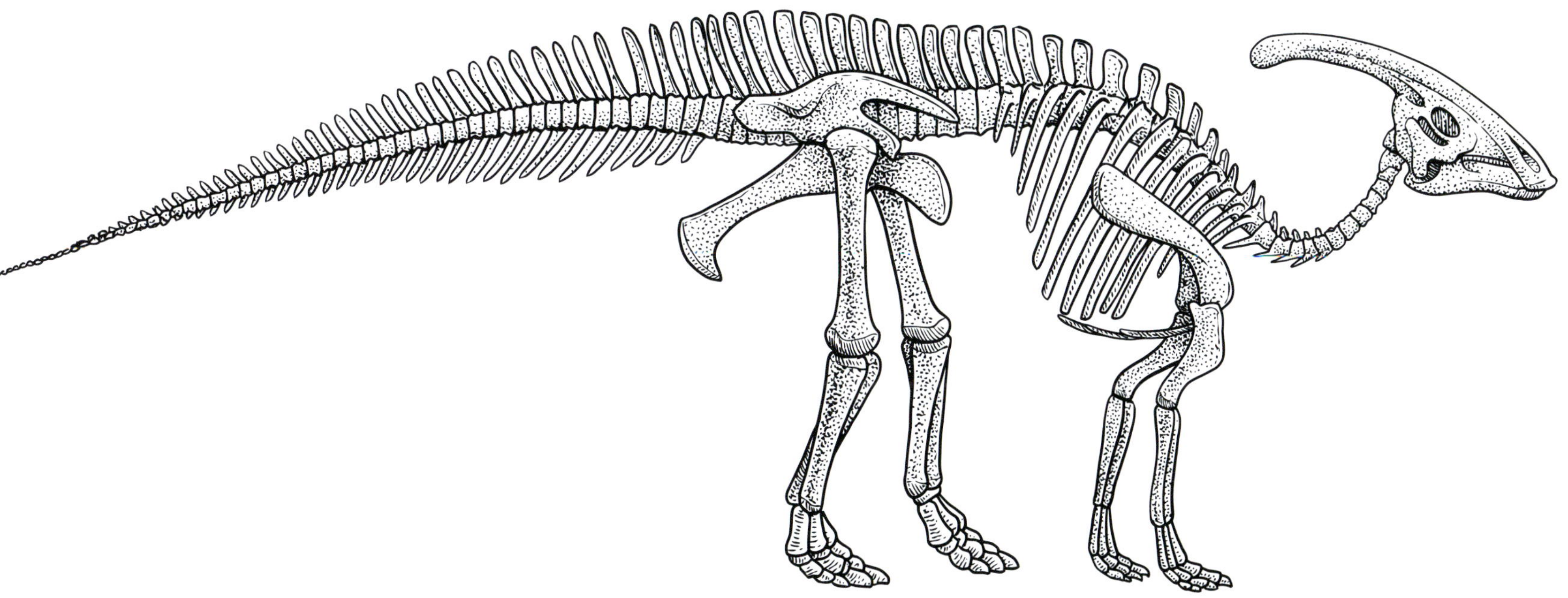

Abdo Kids Jumbo is an Imprint of Abdo Kids
abdobooks.com

abdobooks.com

Published by Abdo Kids, a division of ABDO, P.O. Box 398166, Minneapolis, Minnesota 55439.

Printed in the United States of America, North Mankato, Minnesota.

052025

092025

Photo Credits: Adobe Stock, Alamy, Getty Images, Science Source, Shutterstock

Production Contributors: Teddy Borth, Jennie Forsberg, Grace Hansen
Design Contributors: Candice Keimig, Pakou Moua

Library of Congress Control Number: 2024947606

Publisher's Cataloging-in-Publication Data

Names: Hansen, Grace, author.

Title: Ornithopods: two-footed dinosaurs / by Grace Hansen

Other Title: two-footed dinosaurs

Description: Minneapolis, Minnesota : Abdo Kids, 2026 | Series: Dinosaur groups | Includes online resources and index.

Identifiers: ISBN 9798384905165 (lib. bdg.) | ISBN 9798384905868 (ebook) | ISBN 9798384906216 (read-to-me ebook)

Subjects: LCSH: Dinosaurs--Juvenile literature. | Prehistoric animals--Juvenile literature. | Animals, Fossil--Juvenile literature. | Paleontology--Juvenile literature.

Classification: DDC 567.90--dc23

Table of Contents

The Two-Footed Dinosaurs

Ornithopods were a group of dinosaurs. They lived from the Middle Jurassic to the Late Cretaceous. They were found throughout the world.

Jurassic

201 million years ago

Cretaceous

145 million years ago

Ornithopods

The group's name means "bird feet." Members had three-toed, birdlike feet.

Pigeon feet

There were two main groups of ornithopods. Small ornithopods could be the size of a dog. Large ornithopods could be bigger than a bus!

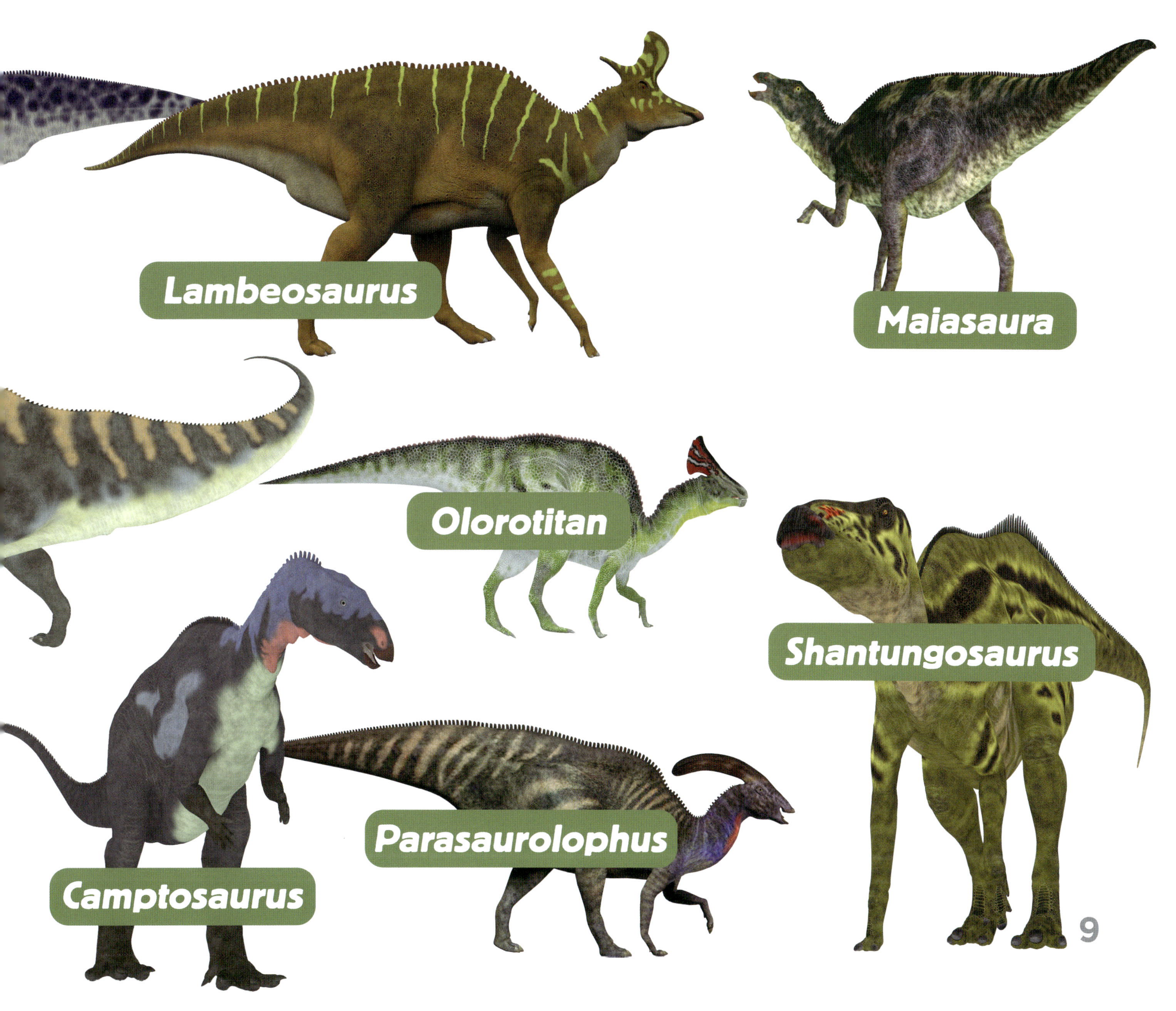
Lambeosaurus
Maiasaura
Olorotitan
Shantungosaurus
Camptosaurus
Parasaurolophus

Smaller members of the group walked on two legs. Larger dinosaurs mainly walked on four legs. They could stand on their **hind limbs** to reach food in trees.

Ornithopods were **herbivores**. They had special teeth for chewing tough plants. Later members had a duck-billed mouth that helped with plucking food.

Leaellynasaura

Leaellynasaura was a small ornithopod. It had a very long tail for its body size. It likely had feathers to keep it warm.

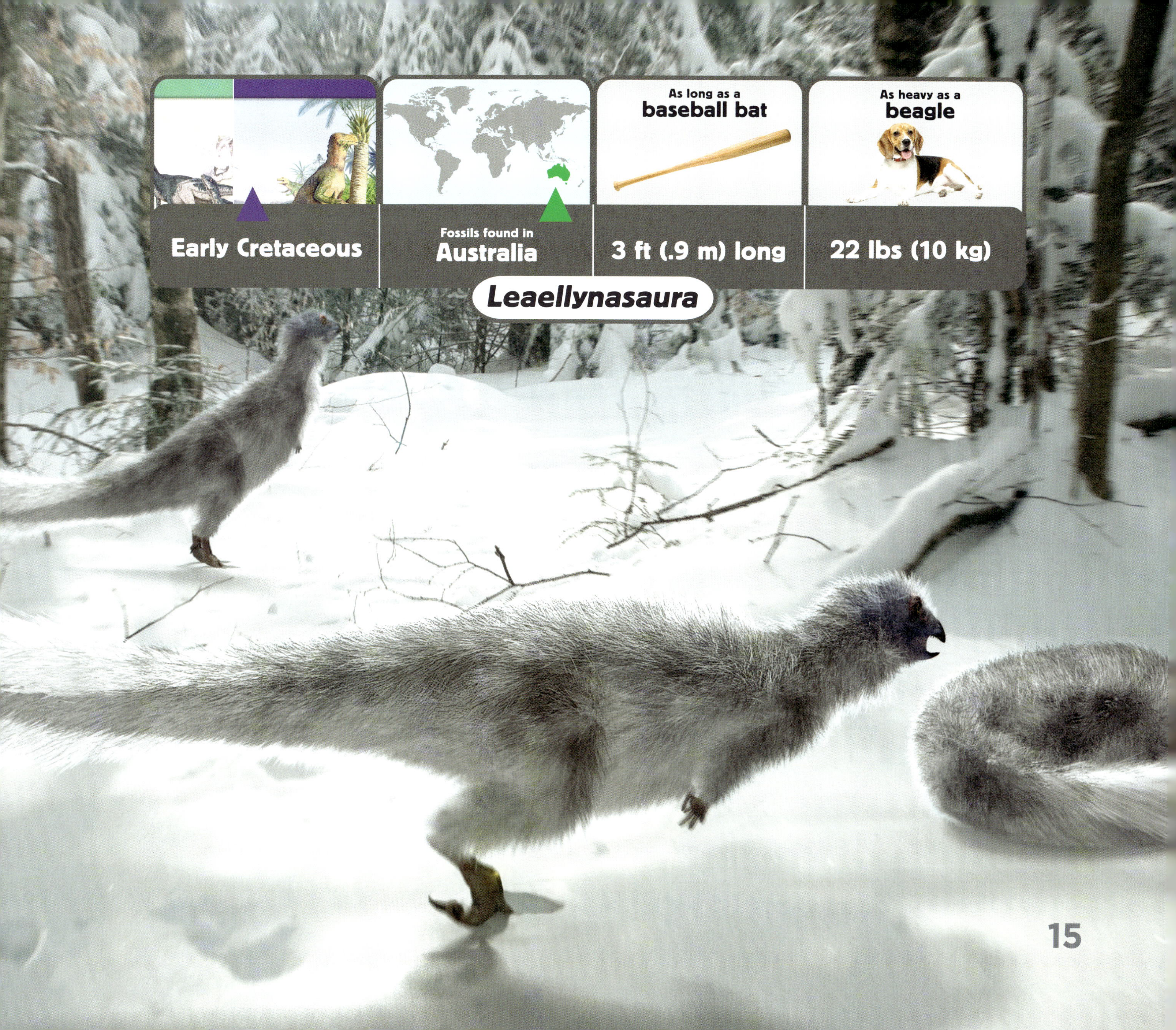
Early Cretaceous
Fossils found in
Australia
As long as a
baseball bat
3 ft (.9 m) long
As heavy as a
beagle
22 lbs (10 kg)
Leaellynasaura

Camptosaurus

Camptosaurus was a large ornithopod. It had very strong **hind limbs**. It may have been able to run about 15 mph (25 km/h).

Late Jurassic
Fossils found in
North America
and Europe
As long as a
great hammerhead
16 ft (5 m)
As heavy as
2 quarter horses
2,200 lbs
(1,000 kg)
Camptosaurus

Parasaurolophus

Parasaurolophus was a large ornithopod. It was known for its large head **crest**. It could blow air through its crest to make noise.

Parasaurolophus
Late Cretaceous
Fossils found in
North America
As long as a
stretch limo
30 ft
(9 m)
As heavy as an
Asian elephant
8,000 lbs
(3,600 kg)

Shantungosaurus

Shantungosaurus was maybe the largest ornithopod to ever live. It had about 1,500 tiny chewing teeth. It also had a large hole near its **nostrils**. This was likely used to make noise.

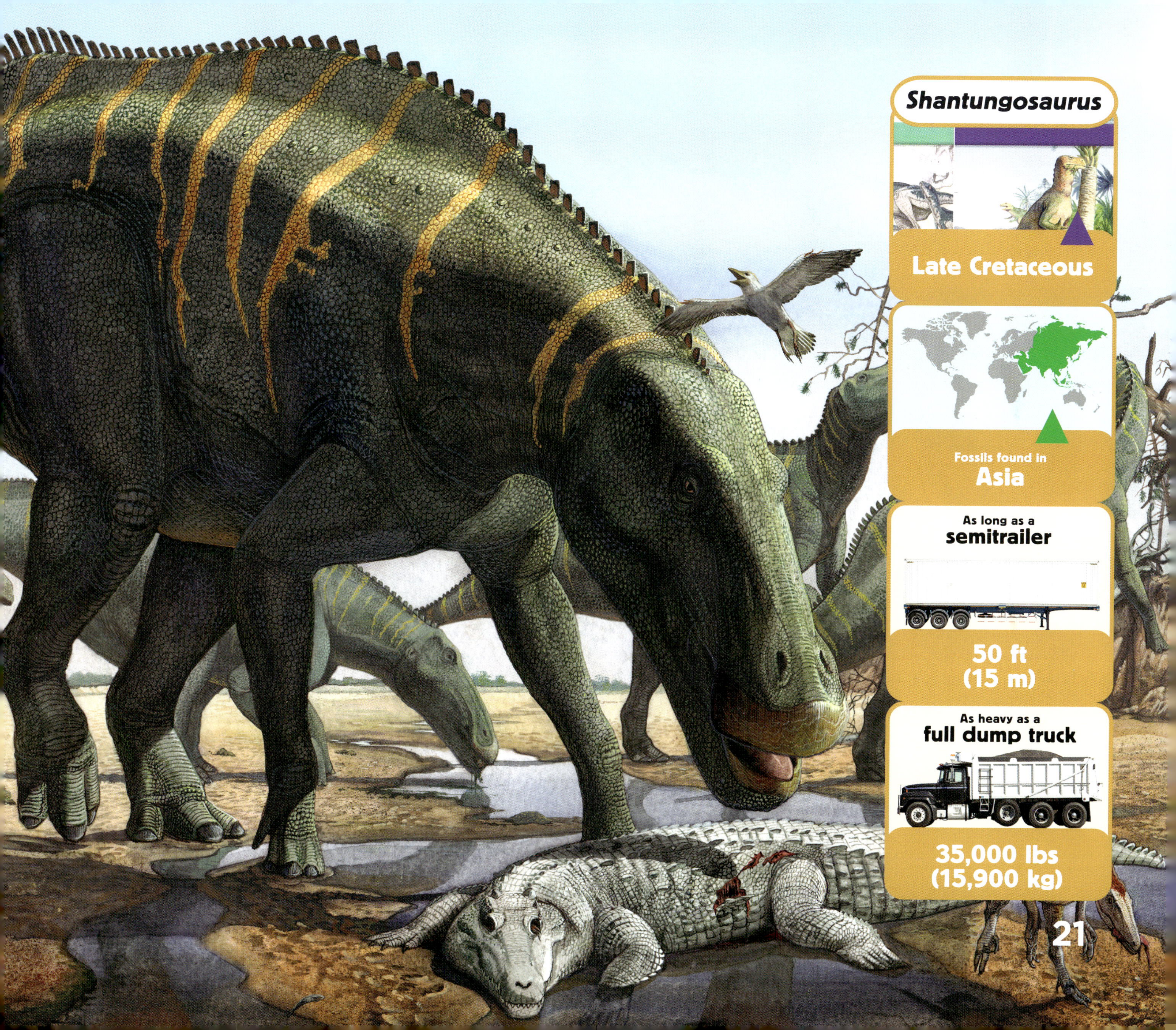

Shantungosaurus
Late Cretaceous
Fossils found in
Asia
As long as a
semitrailer
50 ft
(15 m)
As heavy as a
full dump truck
35,000 lbs
(15,900 kg)

Common Ornithopod Features

Early Ornithopods

- Smaller in size
- Mainly moved on two legs
- Fast
- Three-toed feet
- Stiff tail for balance

Later Ornithopods

- Large in size
- Mainly moved on four legs
- Strong, sturdy body
- Many chewing teeth
- Three-toed feet
- Some members had a duck-billed mouth

Glossary

crest – a tuft of feathers, bone, or fur on an animal's head.

herbivore – an animal that only feeds on plants.

hind limb – a moving, bending part on the back of the body. A back leg is a hind limb.

nostril – one of the two outside openings in the nose.

Index

Visit **abdokids.com** to access crafts, games, videos, and more!

Use Abdo Kids code

DOK5165

or scan this QR code!